HERE'S WHAT HAPPENED!

Donald Gorbach

ISBN-10 1979842469
ISBN-13 978-1979842464

" I DOUBT THAT MANY PEOPLE READING THIS
WILL EVER LOSE A PRESIDENTIAL ELECTION
(ALTHOUGH MAYBE SOME HAVE:
HI AL, JOHN, HI MITT, HOPE YOU'RE WELL.)"

—HILLARY RODHAM CLINTON

REALITYCOVERBOOKS.COM